Envision It! | Visual Skills Handbook

Compare and Contrast

Draw Conclusions

Main Idea and Details

Sequence

Literary Elements

EI•1

Compare and Contrast

Draw Conclusions

= Happy

Main Idea and Details

Main Idea

Details

Sequence

Literary Elements

Characters

BROTHER
MOMMY
DADDY
SISTER

Setting

Theme

Plot

Beginning

Middle

End

Envision It! | Visual Strategies Handbook

Background Knowledge

Let's Think About Reading!

- What do I already know?
- What does this remind me of?

Important Ideas

Let's **Think** About **Reading!**

- What is important to know?

Inferring

Let's Think About Reading!

- What do I already know?
- How does this help me understand what happened?

Monitor and Clarify

Let's Think About Reading!

- What does not make sense?
- How can I fix it?

Predict and Set Purpose

Let's Think About Reading!

- What do I already know?
- What do I think will happen?
- What is my purpose for reading?

Questioning

Let's Think About Reading!

- What questions do I have about what I am reading?

Story Structure

Beginning

Middle

End

Let's Think About Reading!

- What happens in the beginning?
- What happens in the middle?
- What happens in the end?

Summarize

The dog knocked over the table.

Let's Think About Reading!

- What happens in the story?
- What is the story mainly about?

Text Structure

Let's **Think** About **Reading!**

- How is the story organized?
- Are there any patterns?

Visualize

Let's **Think** About **Reading!**

- What pictures do I see in my mind?

SCOTT FORESMAN
READING STREET

GRADE 1

COMMON CORE ©

Program Authors

Peter Afflerbach

Camille Blachowicz

Candy Dawson Boyd

Elena Izquierdo

Connie Juel

Edward Kame'enui

Donald Leu

Jeanne R. Paratore

P. David Pearson

Sam Sebesta

Deborah Simmons

Susan Watts Taffe

Alfred Tatum

Sharon Vaughn

Karen Kring Wixson

Glenview, Illinois

Boston, Massachusetts

Chandler, Arizona

Upper Saddle River, New Jersey

ALWAYS LEARNING

PEARSON

We dedicate Reading Street to
Peter Jovanovich.

His wisdom, courage,
and passion for education
are an inspiration to us all.

Accelerated Reader®

Acknowledgments appear on page 258, which constitutes an extension of this copyright page.

ISBN-13: 978-0-328-72448-2
ISBN-10:   0-328-72448-3
2 3 4 5 6 7 8 9 10 V042 16 15 14 13 12

Dear Reader,

Scott Foresman Reading Street has many corners and crossroads. At each corner you will learn about something new and interesting. You will read about great ideas in science and social studies. You will have fun reading about clever chicks and smart mouse detectives!

You may want to hurry down the street and read these wonderful stories and articles! But slow down, take your time, and enjoy yourself! You never know who you might meet on *Reading Street!*

Sincerely,
The Authors

Great Ideas

What difference can a great idea make?

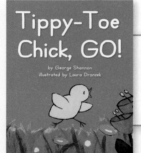

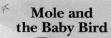

Unit 5 Contents

Week 6

Envision It! A Comprehension Handbook

Envision It! Visual Skills Handbook EI•1–EI•7

Envision It! Visual Strategies Handbook EI•9–EI•19

Don Leu
The Internet Guy

Right before our eyes, the nature of reading and learning is changing. The Internet and other technologies create new opportunities, new solutions, and new literacies. New reading comprehension skills are required online. They are increasingly important to our students and our society.

Those of us on the Reading Street team are here to help you on this new, and very exciting, journey.

See It!

- **Big Question Video**

- **Concept Talk Video**

- **Envision It! Animations**

- **eReaders**

- **Interactive Sound-Spelling Cards**

Hear It!

- *Sing with Me* **Animations**

- **eSelections**

- **Grammar Jammer**

- **Vocabulary Activities**

Concept Talk Video

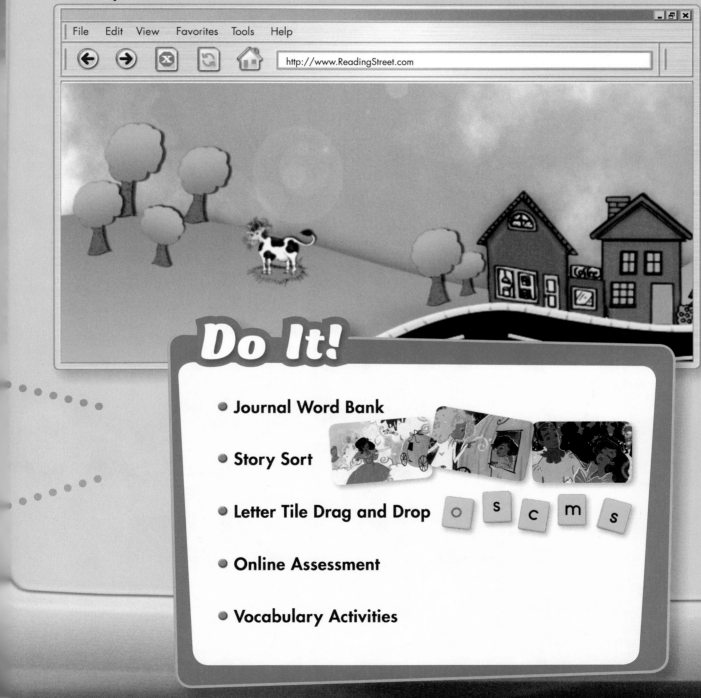

File   Edit   View   Favorites   Tools   Help

http://www.ReadingStreet.com

Do It!

- **Journal Word Bank**

- **Story Sort**

- **Letter Tile Drag and Drop**

- **Online Assessment**

- **Vocabulary Activities**

Great Ideas

THE BIG ?

What difference can a great idea make?

Read Together

Let's Talk About

Clever Solutions

- With a partner or in a group, discuss what is happening in the photographs on these pages. Listen to others to understand things in the photographs that you already know and things that you don't know anything about.

- Share information about great ideas and clever solutions.

- Discuss problems we might encounter.

- Share ideas about when a problem needs a clever solution.

READING STREET ONLINE
CONCEPT TALK VIDEO
www.ReadingStreet.com

Phonemic Awareness

Let's Listen for

Sounds

Read Together

- Find the picture of the table. Remove the sound /t/ from the beginning of *table*. Say the new word.

- Find something that rhymes with *now*. Say the sound at the beginning of the word.

- Find something that rhymes with *town*. Say the sound at the end of the word.

- Find an animal that has a shell. Say each sound in the animal's name.

READING STREET ONLINE
SOUND-SPELLING CARDS
www.ReadingStreet.com

Common Core State Standards

Foundational Skills 3. Know and apply grade-level phonics and word analysis skills in decoding words.
Also Foundational Skills 3.g.

Envision It! **Sounds to Know**

owl

ow

mouse

ou

Phonics

Diphthongs *ow, ou*

Words I Can Blend

| p | r | ou | d |

| t | ow | n |

| c | r | ow | d |

| l | ou | d |

| f | ou | n | d |

Sentences I Can Read

1. We're proud of this town.

2. Is that crowd too loud?

3. Jenny found a red stone.

Words I Can Read

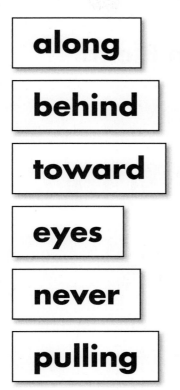

Sentences I Can Read

1. That farmer walked along behind his plow.

2. My eyes look toward those clouds.

3. We never used the brown cow for pulling that cart.

Common Core State Standards
Foundational Skills 3.e. Decode two-syllable words following basic patterns by breaking the words into syllables.
Also Foundational Skills 3., 3.g.

Envision It! Sounds to Know

candle

syllable -le

READING STREET ONLINE
SOUND-SPELLING CARDS
www.ReadingStreet.com

Phonics

Final Syllable -le

Words I Can Blend

p u z z l e

t a b l e

p u r p l e

a p p l e

a b l e

Sentences I Can Read

1. We left my puzzle on that table.

2. Tish has a purple plum and a red apple.

3. Is Justin able to run fast?

Turtle walked south along the streets of town, pulling a bundle of sticks behind him. He planned to make a little house with these sticks. Eagle flew down from cloudy skies toward Turtle.

"May I take a few sticks in my mouth to make a nest?" asked Eagle nicely. "I can handle five or six."

Turtle blinked his eyes. "Yes," he said. "I will never say no to a gentle pal."

Tippy-Toe

by George Shannon

illustrated by Laura Dronzek

 **Genre** The animal characters in an **animal fantasy** act like people. In the next story you will read about a smart little chick who has a great idea. What do you want to find out? Set a purpose for reading.

Then running, *tippy-toe, tippy-toe,* to
catch the rest. Across the yard. Into the
garden to eat, eat, eat. Every day, every day
of the week.

Till ONE day—

RUFF-RUFF-RUFF-RUFF-RUFF!

A big, grumpy dog came running their way,
barking and growling at the end of a rope.

Hen jumped back and pulled her chicks
near. "There's no safe way to the beans today.
We'll just have to wait for chicken feed."

All three chicks said, "Bleck!" and frowned.

"We're hungry!"

"You PROMISED!"

"We DID our chores!"

Hen sighed. "But we'll NEVER get past a dog like that."

Big Chick said, "Wait. I'LL take care of this."
He slowly took a step toward Dog. "Now listen,"
he called. "We won't hurt you. We're just going
to the garden for an itty-bitty treat."

RUFF-RUFF-RUFF-RUFF-RUFF!

Dog disagreed, barking and pulling at the end of his rope. Big Chick ran to hide under Hen's safe wing.

Middle Chick took a breath, then stepped toward Dog. "I'M hungry, so YOU'D better stop it right now! Or YOU'LL be sorry when we get hold of you."

RUFF-RUFF-RUFF-RUFF-RUFF!

Dog disagreed, barking and pulling at the end of his rope. Middle Chick ran to hide under Hen's safe wing.

"Let's go," said Hen. "We'll really have to wait."

Little Chick peeped, "*I* want to try."

"Oh, no!" said Hen, as the other chicks laughed. "You're much too small."

Little Chick yelled, "But *I* can RUN!" And off she went, *tippy-toe, tippy-toe,* as fast as she could. Straight toward Dog.

Hen screamed and grabbed her heart.

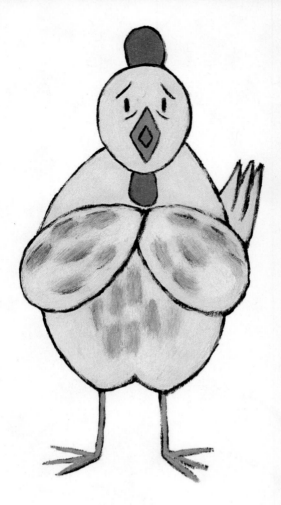

Big Chick closed his eyes.

Middle Chick shook.

Little Chick ran, *tippy-toe, tippy-toe*, without stopping to rest till she felt Dog's breath.

Then Little Chick laughed and began to run again. *Tippy-toe, tippy-toe* around the tree.

Dog chased after her, tugging at his rope.
RUFF-RUFF-RUFF-RUFF-RUFF!

Tippy-toe, tippy-toe around the tree. *Tippy-toe, tippy-toe, tippy* . . . **RUFF-RUFF-RUFF!**

Around and around, *tippy-toe, tippy-toe.* Till . . .

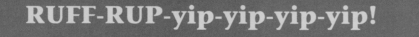

RUFF-RUP-yip-yip-yip-yip!

Dog's rope was wrapped all around the tree. He was stuck and too mad to think "back up."

Hen clucked with pride. Big Chick and Middle Chick just stood and stared.

Little Chick called, "It's time to eat!"

And off they ran, *tippy-toe, tippy-toe*. Right past Dog and into the garden for their favorite treat—sweet itty-bitty beans and potato bugs.

"YUM!"

Common Core State Standards
Literature 1. Ask and answer questions
about key details in a text. Also Writing 8.

Think Critically

Read Together

Envision It! Retell

**READING STREET ONLINE
STORY SORT**
www.ReadingStreet.com

1. How can being little be helpful? Text to World

2. Why does the author let the smallest chick save the day? Think Like an Author

3. What words would you use to describe Little Chick? Where does she live?

   Character, Setting, and Plot

4. As you read the story, did anything confuse you? What did you do?

   Monitor and Clarify

5. **Look Back and Write**
   Look back at pages 34–37. Why was Little Chick's idea great? Write about it. Use evidence from the story to support your answer. Discuss what you wrote with a partner.

   Key Ideas and Details • Text Evidence

George Shannon

George Shannon is a tall man, but he likes little things. One of his favorite sayings is "Less is more." Does that sound like a good lesson for Little Chick?

Mr. Shannon likes to tell stories. He says, "I want my stories to sound as if they are being told out loud."

Here are other books by George Shannon.

SEEDS
GEORGE SHANNON
ILLUSTRATED BY STEVE BJÖRKMAN

Lizard's Guest

Use the Reading Log in the *Reader's and Writer's Notebook* to record your independent reading.

Reading Log

Common Core State Standards

Writing 3. Write narratives in which they recount two or more appropriately sequenced events, include some details regarding what happened, use temporal words to signal event order, and provide some sense of closure. **Also Language 1.j.**

Let's Write It!

Read Together

Key Features of an Animal Fantasy

- characters are animals
- animals do things that real animals cannot do

READING STREET ONLINE
GRAMMAR JAMMER
www.ReadingStreet.com

Narrative

Animal Fantasy

An **animal fantasy** is a made-up story about animals doing things that people do. The student model on the next page is an example of an animal fantasy.

Writing Prompt Think of a problem that needs a solution. Now write an animal fantasy that tells how animals solve the problem.

Writer's Checklist

Remember, you should . . .

☑ have animals do things that real animals cannot do.

☑ show animals solving a problem.

☑ use an imperative sentence.

The Big Problem

Little Mouse wanted cheese.

Cat was in the kitchen.

Little Mouse remembered. Big Mouse had said what to do.

Wait until Cat is sleeping. Grab a bit of cheese. Run!

Little Mouse did.

Genre Animal Fantasy
The mice talk and think like people.

Writing Trait Voice
The author shows interest in Little Mouse.

In these **imperative sentences**, Big Mouse tells Little Mouse what to do. Say them in a strong voice.

Conventions

● **Imperative Sentences**

Remember An **imperative sentence** tells someone what to do. Say this sentence.
Come back, Little Chick.

Genre
Folk Tale

- A folk tale is a well-known story that people have told through the years.

- A folk tale often has animal characters that speak and act like people. The animals have a problem they must solve.

- Sometimes words or actions are repeated in a folk tale.

- Sometimes we can connect the meaning of a folk tale to our own experiences.

- Read "Little Red Hen." Look for elements that make it a folk tale.

- If you come to a part you don't understand, remember to reread that part aloud to help you make sense of what you're reading.

Little Red Hen

retold by Odette Calderón
illustrated by Constanza Basaluzzo

Read Together

One day Little Red Hen was scratching the ground near her house. "Who will help me plant this grain of wheat I found?"

"Not I," said Cat, Pig,
and Duck together.
"I must do it myself,"
sighed Little Red Hen.

Let's Think About...

Who are the characters in this story? How are they different from real animals?
Folk Tale

45

Let's Think About...

Who is the main character in this story? How is she different from the other characters?
Folk Tale

Soon the wheat was tall and golden. Little Red Hen cut the wheat and took it to the miller. The miller ground it into flour.

46

"Who will help me bake a muffin?"
"Not I," said Cat, Pig, and Duck.
"I must do it myself," sighed Little
Red Hen.

Let's **Think** About...

What words on this page have been said before in the story? **Folk Tale**

Let's Think About...

What do Cat, Pig, and Duck say now? How is this different from what they said before? **Folk Tale**

Soon the soft brown muffin was ready. "Who will help me eat this muffin?"

"I will!" cried Cat, Pig, and Duck together.

"You will not!" said Little Red Hen.
And she ate the tasty muffin herself.

Let's **Think** About...

What is the meaning of this folk tale? How can you connect it to something that has happened to you? **Folk Tale**

Let's **Think** About...

Reading Across Texts What problem do the hen and chicks in *Tippy-Toe Chick, GO!* have? What problem does the hen in "Little Red Hen" have? How do the characters solve their problems?

Writing Across Texts Write about what happens to Dog in *Tippy-Toe Chick, GO!* and to Cat, Pig, and Duck in "Little Red Hen."

49

Common Core State Standards
Language 5. With guidance and support from adults, demonstrate understanding of word relationships and nuances in word meanings. **Also Foundational Skills 4.b.**

Let's Learn It!

Read Together

**READING STREET ONLINE
VOCABULARY ACTIVITIES**
www.ReadingStreet.com

Get Ready For Grade 2

Listen for sound and watch for movement that can make a program seem more real.

Media Literacy

Techniques in Media Some types of media, such as television, use sound and movement. This helps us better understand what we are hearing and watching. It makes us feel as if we are there.

Practice It! Imagine you are watching a scene from a movie in which a rocket is blasting off into space. What sounds would you hear? What movement would you see?

Vocabulary

A **synonym** is a word that means the same or almost the same as another word.

The girl *smiles*.

The girl *grins*.

Smiles and *grins* are synonyms.

Practice It! Read these words. Write and say a synonym for each word.

quick   nice   tiny   damp

Fluency

Accuracy, Rate, and Expression
When you read, try to read with no mistakes. Read the sentences as if you were talking. Use your voice to add emotion.

Practice It!

1. Our house is along the edge of town.

2. Pulling the bag toward me was hard.

Oral Vocabulary

Let's Talk About

Read Together

Clever Solutions

- Share information about great ideas and clever solutions.

- Share ideas about how we can look at things in a different way.

READING STREET ONLINE
CONCEPT TALK VIDEO
www.ReadingStreet.com

Common Core State Standards

Foundational Skills 2.d. Segment spoken single-syllable words into their complete sequence of individual sounds (phonemes).

Phonemic Awareness

Let's Listen for

Sounds

Read Together

- The clown is holding a pouch. Remove the sound /p/ from the beginning of *pouch*. Say the new word.

- Find three things that rhyme with *brown*. Say the sound in the middle of those words.

- There are three crows in the street. Say each sound in the word *crows*.

READING STREET ONLINE
SOUND-SPELLING CARDS
www.ReadingStreet.com

Common Core State Standards
Foundational Skills 3. Know and apply
grade-level phonics and word analysis skills
in decoding words.
Also Foundational Skills 3.g.

Envision It! | Sounds to Know

snow

ow

owl

ow

soup

ou

mouse

ou

shoulder

ou

READING STREET ONLINE
SOUND-SPELLING CARDS
www.ReadingStreet.com

Phonics

🔄 Vowel Patterns
OW, OU

Words I Can Blend

sh ow

h ow

y ou

ou t

sh ou l d e r

Sentences I Can Read

1. Please show me how
to play.

2. Will you take me out
for dinner?

3. Martin hurt his shoulder
when he fell.

Words I Can Read

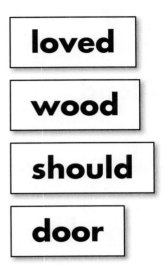

loved

wood

should

door

Sentences I Can Read

1. Sam loved sitting on the brown boulder.

2. Should I throw that wood on the fire?

3. Can you close that door?

Common Core State Standards
Foundational Skills 3.e. Decode
two-syllable words following basic
patterns by breaking the words into
syllables. **Also Foundational Skills 3., 3.g.**

Envision It! Sounds to Know

tiger

V/CV

lemon

VC/V

READING STREET ONLINE
SOUND-SPELLING CARDS
www.ReadingStreet.com

Phonics

Syllables V/CV, VC/V

Words I Can Blend

b a b y

n e v e r

o p e n

f i n i sh

l a t e r

Sentences I Can Read

1. The baby is sleeping.

2. Never open that gate when our dog is near.

3. You can finish reading that book later.

How do you help at home? Do you ever throw out trash? Can you help pick up **wood** sticks in the yard when Dad or Mom mows?

Maybe you make sure you always close the **door** after you open it. Or you take your shower without being asked.

Kids are **loved**, but they **should** show they care too.

In an **animal fantasy**, the animal characters talk and act like people. The next story is about a mole who finds and takes care of a baby bird.

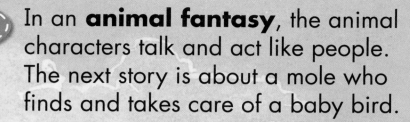

Mole and the Baby Bird

by Marjorie Newman

illustrated by Patrick Benson

Question of the Week

How can we look at things in a different way?

Mole found a baby bird.
It had fallen out of its nest.

Mole waited and waited: but no
big bird came to help it—so Mole
took the baby bird home.

He made a nest for it.
"Look!" he said to his mother.

"It's very, very hard to take care of a baby
bird," she said.

"They usually die," said his dad.

"My bird won't die," said Mole.

His friends helped him find food
for the baby.

His mother showed him how to feed
it. Mole fed it whenever it chirped.

And the bird didn't die! It grew.
"It's my pet bird," said Mole.
"It's not a pet bird. It's a wild bird,"
said his mother.

The bird fluttered its wings.

"Your bird is trying to fly," said his mother.

"No!" cried Mole. "It mustn't fly!"

Mole found some wood and some nails.
He borrowed his dad's toolbox.

"What are you making?" asked his dad.
"I'm making a cage for my pet bird!"
said Mole.

"It's not a pet bird. It's a wild bird,"
said his dad. "You should let it fly."
"No!" cried Mole.

He put his bird into its new cage.
The bird was sad.

Mole's mother was sad too. But Mole
kept his bird, because he loved it.

Then—Grandad came to visit. He looked at
Mole's pet bird.

Presently Grandad said, "Let's go for a walk,
little Mole."

Grandad took Mole to the top of a high hill.

Mole looked down at the trees far below.

He felt the wild wind trying to lift him.
"Wheee! I'm flying!" cried Mole.
"Nearly," said Grandad.

When Mole got home he looked at his bird.
It was sitting very still in its cage in Mole's dark
underground room. "Birds are meant to fly,"
said Mole.

He opened the cage door, and he let his bird
fly away because he loved it. Then he cried.

The next day Mole went into the forest.
He saw his bird flying, soaring, free. And Mole
was glad.

Common Core State Standards
Literature 1. Ask and answer questions about key details in a text. **Also Literature 2., Writing 5.**

Envision It! | Retell

READING STREET ONLINE
STORY SORT
www.ReadingStreet.com

Think Critically

1. What lesson did Mole learn? Was it a good lesson to learn? Why do you think so? Text to World

2. Why do you think the author wrote this story? Author's Purpose

3. Why was the baby bird sad? Draw Conclusions

4. What do you know about taking care of pets that helped you understand this story? Background Knowledge

5. Look Back and Write Look back at page 74. Why does Mole think he is flying? Provide evidence to support your answer.

Key Ideas and Details • Text Evidence

Meet the Author and the Illustrator

Marjorie Newman

Marjorie Newman lives in England. As a child, she often brought home caterpillars and tadpoles. When they turned into butterflies and frogs, she let them go.

Patrick Benson

Patrick Benson tries to show different views in his art. Can you find a picture that shows how the world looks to a flying bird?

Here are other books written by Marjorie Newman or illustrated by Patrick Benson.

Use the Reading Log in the *Reader's and Writer's Notebook* to record your independent reading.

79

Common Core State Standards

Writing 2. Write informative/explanatory texts in which they name a topic, supply some facts about the topic, and provide some sense of closure. **Also Literature 4., Language 1.d.**

Let's Write It!

Read Together

Key Features of a Letter to a Character

- describes feelings to a story character
- includes a friendly greeting and closing

READING STREET ONLINE
GRAMMAR JAMMER
www.ReadingStreet.com

Expressive

Letter to a Character

A **letter to a character** can express your feelings about the character or story. The student model on the next page is an example of a letter to a character.

Writing Prompt Think about how Mole changed his mind. Write a letter to Mole. Tell him how you feel about the way he helped the bird at the end.

Writer's Checklist

Remember, you should . . .

☑ write to Mole about what he did in the story.

☑ tell your feelings.

☑ use a few pronouns in your sentences.

Dear Mole,

   It was nice of you to let the bird fly.

   I think a bird needs to go out.

   You were a good friend to it.

   You can get a new pet.

                Your fan,
                Tom

**Genre
Letter**
The letter has a greeting and a closing.

**Writing Trait
Voice**
The letter shows the author's feelings. The pronoun *I* is capitalized.

The **pronoun
you** takes the place of Mole's name.

Conventions

● **Pronouns**

   Remember The words **I, you, he, she, it, we,** and **they** are pronouns.

      The birds can fly.   **They** can fly.

Common Core State Standards
Literature 3. Describe characters, settings, and major events in a story, using key details. **Also Literature 9.**

Brave
Little Cuckoo

Read Together

Genre
Folk Tale

- A folk tale often has animal characters that speak and act like people. The main character has a problem to solve.

- When a folk tale begins with the phrase "Once upon a time," it means that people have been telling it a long time.

- When a folk tale ends with the phrase "They lived happily ever after," it means that things turn out all right for the characters.

- As you read "Brave Little Cuckoo," look for elements of a folk tale.

- If you come to a part you don't understand, use what you know to make a picture in your head to help you understand what you're reading.

Once upon a time, long before there were cities and roads, Cuckoo flew through a forest in Mexico.

Cuckoo had shining feathers in shades of red, green, yellow, and blue. She also had the most beautiful voice in the forest.

Let's Think About...

How does the story begin? What does that phrase tell you? **Folk Tale**

83

How is Blackbird
different from real
blackbirds?
Folk Tale

"Be quiet, Cuckoo!" chirped Blackbird. "Come help us gather seeds!" But Cuckoo just kept singing. The other birds kept working.

After the other animals went to sleep, Cuckoo saw a fire coming. It would burn up all the seeds! What should she do? Then she saw Mole in his hole in the ground. Cuckoo had an idea.

Let's Think About...

What is Cuckoo's problem? How do you think she will solve it? **Folk Tale**

Let's **Think** About...

How did Cuckoo solve her problem?
Folk Tale

Cuckoo carried all the seeds to Mole's hole so they would not burn. The seeds were saved! But the soot made Cuckoo's colorful feathers black. The smoke made her lovely voice scratchy and rough.

The animals in the forest decided that Cuckoo was the bravest bird in the forest. Because of her bravery, now all cuckoos have dull feathers and harsh voices.

Let's **Think** About...

This story does not end with "They lived happily ever after." How would the story's meaning change if that phrase were added? **Folk Tale**

Let's **Think** About...

Reading Across Texts How do Mole in *Mole and the Baby Bird* and Cuckoo in "Brave Little Cuckoo" show that they are brave?

Writing Across Texts Write about the problems that Mole and Cuckoo face and how they solve their problems.

Common Core State Standards
Speaking/Listening 1.a. Follow agreed-upon rules for discussions (e.g., listening to others with care, speaking one at a time about the topics and texts under discussion). **Also Foundational Skills 4.b.**

Let's Learn It!

Read Together

READING STREET ONLINE
VOCABULARY ACTIVITIES
www.ReadingStreet.com

> I took notes so I would remember what I wanted to say. I think the book we read has interesting characters. On page 5 ...

Listening and Speaking

Get Ready For Grade 2

Be prepared for discussions in which we share information and ideas.

Share Information and Ideas When we share information and ideas, it is important to be prepared. Taking notes is one way to be responsible during a discussion.

Practice It! Think of ways to be responsible in a discussion. Take good notes. Tell a partner. Use pronouns. Then use these responsible methods in your next discussion.

Vocabulary

Words in a **dictionary** or **glossary** are in alphabetical order. If the words start with the same letter, look at the second letter.

baby   **bird**   **bun**

The *second letter* of these words helps put them in alphabetical order.

Practice It! Read these words. Write them in alphabetical order.

mole   **mice**   **mask**   **munch**

Fluency

Accuracy, Rate, Expression, and Appropriate Phrasing When you read, try to read with no mistakes. Give your voice feeling. Use the punctuation marks.

Practice It!

1. That music should not be so loud!

2. How can she use wood for the cabin?

3. Tammy loved the way the baby smiled.

Common Core State Standards

Speaking/Listening 1.b. Build on others' talk in conversations by responding to the comments of others through multiple exchanges.

Oral Vocabulary

Let's Talk About

Read Together

Clever Solutions

- Share ideas about the kinds of things we might want to know.

- Contribute to a discussion about how we solve mysteries.

READING STREET ONLINE
CONCEPT TALK VIDEO
www.ReadingStreet.com

90

Phonemic Awareness

Let's Listen for

Sounds

Read Together

- Find the picture of the books. Take away the sound /s/ from the word *books*. Say the new word.

- Find something that rhymes with *stood*. Say the sound in the middle of the word. Now say the sound at the end.

- The animal in the yard raked the leaves. Say each sound in the word *raked*.

Common Core State Standards
Foundational Skills 3. Know and apply grade-level phonics and word analysis skills in decoding words.
Also Foundational Skills 3.g.

Envision It! | Sounds to Know

book

oo

READING STREET ONLINE
SOUND-SPELLING CARDS
www.ReadingStreet.com

Phonics

Vowel Sound in *foot: oo*

Words I Can Blend

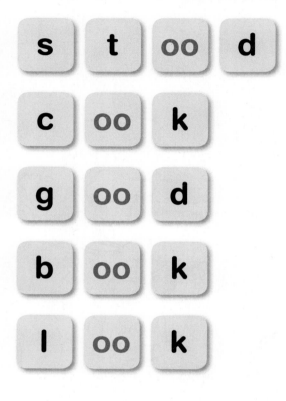

s	t	oo	d
c	oo	k
g	oo	d
b	oo	k
l	oo	k

Sentences I Can Read

1. Dad stood at our stove to cook dinner.

2. That is a good book.

3. Look at that car!

Words I Can Read

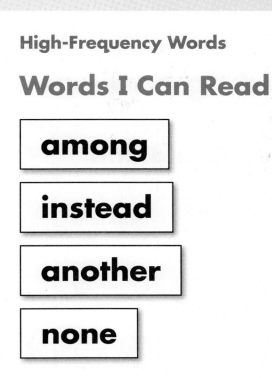

among

instead

another

Sentences I Can Read

1. We found five books among those toys.

2. He made his house from brick instead of wood.

3. None of those kids took another look.

Common Core State Standards
Foundational Skills 3.f. Read words with inflectional endings.
Also Foundational Skills 2.b., 3.g.

Envision It! | Sounds to Know

raced

ending -ed

baking

ending -ing

READING STREET ONLINE
SOUND-SPELLING CARDS
www.ReadingStreet.com

Phonics

Adding Endings

Words I Can Blend

ch a s e s

j o k e d

h i k e d

m a k i ng

h i d i ng

Sentences I Can Read

1. My cat chases her tail.

2. Ben joked with his twin as they hiked.

3. I will be making Kathy a card and hiding it until her birthday.

Andy and Luke liked trading with one another. Among the things those kids traded were games, books, and skates.

Andy had good games, but he liked Luke's instead. None of Luke's books pleased him as much as Andy's.

Their moms took one look at all those trades and said, "That's enough!"

You've learned

- Vowel Sound in *foot*: oo
- Adding Endings

High-Frequency Words

among   instead

another   none

Dot & Jabber
and the Great Acorn Mystery

by Ellen Stoll Walsh

 Read Together

Informational fiction tells a make-believe story, but it also gives facts and information. The next story is a mystery about trees and how they grow where they do.

Question of the Week

How do we solve mysteries?

The detectives had nothing to do.

"We need a mystery to solve," said Jabber.

"Here's a mystery," said Dot. "What is this little oak tree doing here?"

"Why is that a mystery?" Jabber wanted
to know.

"Because of the acorn," said Dot. "How
did it get here?"

"Dot," said Jabber, "what acorn?"

"Acorns are oak tree seeds. This little oak tree grew from an acorn, and acorns come from big oak trees."

"Oh, *that* acorn," said Jabber. "But where's the big oak tree?"

"That's part of the mystery," said Dot. "Let's look for clues."

"Okay!" shouted Jabber. "Because we're detectives!" He poked his head into a hole.

"Hey, this is *my* hole," said a mole. "Go
away. There are no clues down here. Try the
big oak tree—on the *other* side of the meadow."

"Of course!" said Dot. "Come on, Jabber!"

"That's a long, long way," said Jabber.
"How did our acorn get from there to here?
Do you think it walked?"

"Let's find out," said Dot. "The acorn began at the big oak tree. So will we."

The detectives set off across the meadow.

After a while Jabber said, "I'm tired. Can we wonder about all these maple seeds instead?"

"There's no mystery in maple seeds," said Dot. "They have wings that twirl, and they ride the wind across the meadow."

"Maybe our acorn rode the wind too," said Jabber.

"That is what we are going to find out," said Dot.

At last they arrived at the big oak tree. "Look!" said Dot. "I bet there are a million acorns here."

"They don't have wings," said Jabber.
"But they taste good."
"Don't eat them, Jabber! They're clues."

"Acorns don't have wings, but they might have sneaky feet," said Dot. "Let's keep watch and see if they start to move."

Plip. An acorn dropped from the big oak tree.

Jabber poked it with a stick. "This acorn isn't going anywhere," he said. "None of them are."

A squirrel came and sat down among the acorns.

"Jabber, look!" Dot whispered. "What is he doing?"

"Oh!" gasped Jabber. "He's eating our clue!"

"He can't be," said Dot. "The shell is still on it."

"So why is he stuffing it in his
mouth?" asked Jabber.

The squirrel ran off.

"Oh no, he's stealing the acorn!" the
detectives cried and ran after him.

When the squirrel stopped, they stopped and watched to see what would happen next.

"What's he doing now?" asked Jabber.

"Digging a hole. Look! He's hiding the acorn."

Jabber stared at Dot. "Maybe he's planting it!"

"Of course!" said Dot. "Our acorn crossed the meadow on squirrel feet."

"And got planted by squirrel feet," said Jabber.

"And grew into the little oak tree," said Dot. "The mystery is solved. We are two clever mouse detectives!"

"Hurray!" shouted Jabber. "Now what will we do?"

"Find another mystery," said Dot.

"But I'm hungry," said Jabber. "First let's go eat some of those leftover clues."

Common Core State Standards
Informational Text 1. Ask and answer
questions about key details in a text.
Also Informational Text 2., Writing 8.

Envision It! Retell

**READING STREET ONLINE
STORY SORT**
www.ReadingStreet.com

120

Think Critically

Read
Together

1. What skills do detectives need to solve a mystery?

Text to World

2. Why do you think the author chose to write about this mystery? Author's Purpose

3. How are acorns different from maple tree seeds?

Compare and Contrast

4. Did you reread parts of the story? How did that help you understand it? What do you know about trees and seeds that helped you understand? Monitor and Clarify

5. Look Back and Write
Look back at page 108. How do maple seeds move around? Write about it. Use evidence from the story.

Key Ideas and Details • Text Evidence

Read Together

Ellen Stoll Walsh

Ellen Stoll Walsh grew up in a big family. She was one of ten children! It was fun but noisy. She liked to read books to get away from the noise.

Now Ms. Walsh writes books. She cuts paper to make the art. In her books, she tells stories and teaches facts about the world.

Here are other books by Ellen Stoll Walsh.

Dot & Jabber
and the Mystery of the Missing Stream

Ellen Stoll Walsh

Mouse Magic
Ellen Stoll Walsh

More *color* magic by the creator of *Mouse Paint!*

Reading Log

Use the Reading Log in the *Reader's and Writer's Notebook* to record your independent reading.

Common Core State Standards

Language 1.j. Produce and expand complete simple and compound declarative, interrogative, imperative, and exclamatory sentences in response to prompts. **Also Writing 8., Language 1.d.**

Let's Write It!

Read Together

Key Features of Questions

- many start with the word *who, what, when, where, why,* or *how*
- end with a question mark

READING STREET ONLINE
GRAMMAR JAMMER
www.ReadingStreet.com

Questions

A **question** is a kind of sentence that needs an answer. The student model on the next page is an example of questions and one answer.

Writing Prompt Think about questions that you would like to get answered. Write three questions. Find an answer to one question, and write the answer after that question.

Writer's Checklist

Remember, you should . . .

✓ ask about things you would like to know.

✓ choose clear words.

✓ use a pronoun.

✓ end each question with a question mark.

Where do mice hide food?

How big can oak trees grow?

Do animals outside see me?

I think they do see me and run.

Genre Questions
These ask about things the writer wants to know.

Writing Trait Word Choice
The words make these questions clear.

The **pronouns I** and **me** take the place of the writer's name.

Conventions

● **Pronouns (I and me)**

Remember Use the pronoun **I** as the subject of the sentence. **I** is always capitalized. Use **me** after an action verb.

I see Dot.   Dot helps **me**.

Common Core State Standards

Informational Text 7. Use the illustrations and details in a text to describe its key ideas. **Also Informational Text 1.**

Science in Reading

Read Together

Genre
Expository Text

- Expository text tells about real people, animals, places, or events.

- Expository text has a main idea. Facts or details tell more about the main idea.

- In expository text, photographs often help explain the words.

- Read "Water." Look for elements that make this selection expository text.

- Discuss the details of the experiment and discuss your observations. Think about what you already know about water and what is new to you.

Water

Our class did an experiment. We observed changes in water. Here's what we did.

(1.) We put water in a cup.

(2.) We marked it with a line.

(3.) We waited one week.

(4.) We took notes.

124

We looked at the cup. We drew another line to mark the water. The water went down. Where did it go? None of us knew.

Let's Think About...

What questions could you ask about the text to help you clearly understand the steps in the experiment?
Expository Text

Let's Think About...

What facts or details do you learn on these two pages?
Expository Text

125

Let's **Think** About...

What is the main idea of this selection?
Expository Text

Our teacher said that the water went into the air. It is there, but we can't see it. This is called evaporation.

126

We decided to do another experiment. This time we put the water among the plants instead of in the sun. What will happen? We will check for evaporation in a week.

Let's Think About...

What details does the photograph at the top show that the words do not tell?
Expository Text

Let's Think About...

Reading Across Texts The mice in *Dot & Jabber and the Great Acorn Mystery* and the children in "Water" work to solve mysteries. What questions do Dot and Jabber and the children want to answer?

Writing Across Texts Write about what Dot and Jabber find out. Write about what the children find out. What do they all want to do next?

127

Common Core State Standards
Foundational Skills 4.b. Read on-level text orally with accuracy, appropriate rate, and expression on successive readings.
Also Language 5.a.

Let's

Learn

It!

Read Together

Get Ready For Grade 2

Identify sound techniques in order to better understand some media.

Media Literacy

Techniques in Media Some media, such as radio and television, can use sound to describe actions, events, or scenes that we can't see. Sound can help us better understand media.

Practice It! Imagine you are making a radio program. What sounds would you use to describe what is listed below? Share ideas with a partner.

a lion   **a stormy day**   **a busy city**

Vocabulary

Words can be sorted into groups. A **noun** is a person, animal, place, or thing. A **verb** tells what someone or something does.

The boy runs fast.

Boy is a noun.
Runs is a verb.

Practice It! Read each word. Sort these words into two categories—**verbs** and **nouns**.

swim   **girl**   **tree**   **dig**

Fluency

Expression and Intonation When you read, use your voice to make the sentences more interesting.

Practice It!

1. I plan on giving him a book instead.

2. Look, he's making another mess!

3. None of them could cook well.

Common Core State Standards

Speaking/Listening 1.a. Follow agreed-upon rules for discussions (e.g., listening to others with care, speaking one at a time about the topics and texts under discussion).

Oral Vocabulary

Let's Talk About

Ideas That Change Our World

- Discuss ideas that have changed our world.

- Share ideas about how a great idea can make our lives easier.

READING STREET ONLINE
CONCEPT TALK VIDEO
www.ReadingStreet.com

130

Phonemic Awareness

Let's Listen for

Sounds

Read Together

- Find the picture of the soil. Remove the sound /s/ from the word *soil*. Now say the new word.

- Find two things that rhyme with *joy*.

- The singer uses his voice to make music. Say the last sound in *voice*.

READING STREET ONLINE
SOUND-SPELLING CARDS
www.ReadingStreet.com

133

Common Core State Standards
Foundational Skills 3. Know and apply grade-level phonics and word analysis skills in decoding words.
Also Foundational Skills 3.g.

Envision It! Sounds to Know

oil

oi

boy

oy

READING STREET ONLINE
SOUND-SPELLING CARDS
www.ReadingStreet.com

Phonics

Diphthongs *oi, oy*

Words I Can Blend

b oy s

j oi n

p oi n t

t oy

e n j oy s

Sentences I Can Read

1. Boys and girls can join clubs for fun.

2. Point to the toy you like.

3. We hope she enjoys that show.

Words I Can Read

goes

today

kinds

heavy

against

Sentences I Can Read

1. Joy goes to camp today for her first time.

2. These kinds of heavy tools make noise.

3. Troy will lean his toy against that wall.

Common Core State Standards
Foundational Skills 3. Know and apply grade-level phonics and word analysis skills in decoding words.
Also Foundational Skills 3.g.

painter

suffix -er

sailor

suffix -or

READING STREET ONLINE
SOUND-SPELLING CARDS
www.ReadingStreet.com

Phonics

🔊 Suffixes *-er, -or*

Words I Can Blend

t | ea | ch | e | r

p | ai | n | t | e | r

wr | i | t | e | r

v | i | s | i | t | o | r

s | ai | l | o | r

Sentences I Can Read

1. My teacher is a good painter too.

2. That writer is a visitor in my town.

3. A sailor may stay on a ship for weeks.

I Can Read!

This boy Roy is thinking about kinds of jobs. What will he be when he grows up?

Today Dad points out that being a teacher or writer is nice. Mom tells him that he might enjoy being a painter. Joy goes on about an actor she likes.

Roy is not against that. But Roy likes lifting heavy things. He might be a wrestler instead.

You've learned

- Diphthongs *oi, oy*
- Suffixes *-er, -or*

High-Frequency Words
goes   today   kinds
heavy   against

Simple Machines

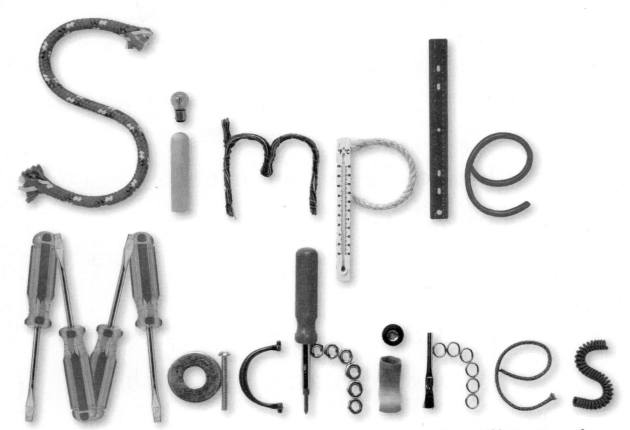

by Allan Fowler

 **Genre**

Expository text explains something. The next selection explains how simple machines make work easier.

Question of the Week

How can a great idea make our lives easier?

We use machines every day. Machines help make our lives easier.

Some machines, such as lawn mowers and vacuum cleaners, have many parts.

vacuum cleaner

lawn mower

Other machines have few parts. They are called simple machines. Levers, inclined planes, wheels and axles, and pulleys are four kinds of simple machines.

These everyday things are simple machines.

This bottle opener is a kind of lever.
It helps you remove the cap from a bottle.

Some levers can help you move a heavy object, such as a rock.

This boy is using a lever called a crowbar.

Push down on one end of a lever. The other end moves up and pushes against whatever you are trying to move.

Have you ever ridden a seesaw?

A seesaw is a kind of lever. One side goes up, while the other side goes down.

Inclined planes are all around you.

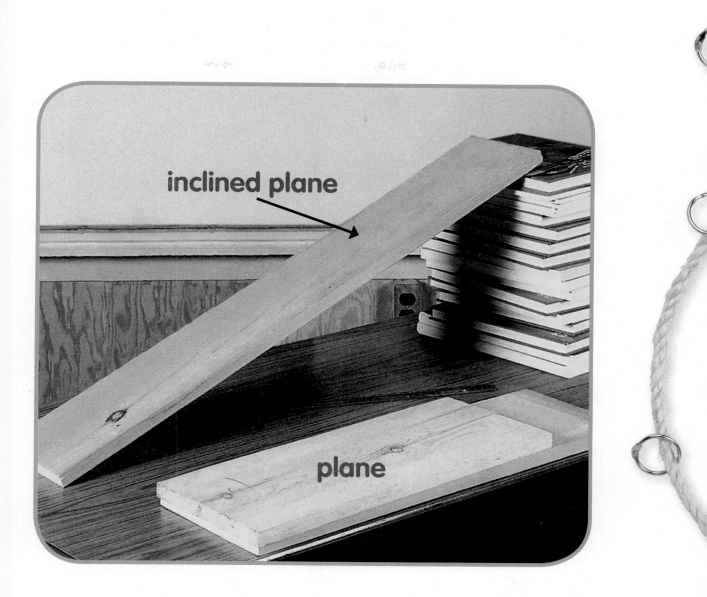

inclined plane

plane

A plane is just a flat surface, like a wooden board. An inclined plane is a flat surface that is slanted.

Ramps are inclined planes. It is easier to push a big load up a ramp than to lift it.

A wedge is another kind
of inclined plane.

wedge

A wedge can help you cut wood.
When a wedge is hit with a big
hammer, its thin part splits the wood.

Wheels help things go.

axle

An axle, or rod, connects a pair of wheels. The axle helps the wheels turn.

Wheels are on bicycles and cars.
It would be very hard to move a bike
or car without wheels.

A pulley helps you lift heavy objects.

pulley

A pulley's rope passes over a small wheel.
Pull down on one end of the rope. You can lift
a very heavy load tied to the other end.

A pulley can help you raise and lower the flag on a flagpole.

You can even lift the sail on a boat using a pulley.

coil of rope

These children are using two kinds of simple machines. A wheelbarrow is a kind of lever, and it has wheels.

Have you used any simple machines today?

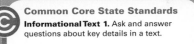

Common Core State Standards
Informational Text 1. Ask and answer questions about key details in a text.

Think Critically

Envision It! Retell

1. What are some simple machines you use in the classroom? Text to Self

2. What does the author want you to learn about simple machines? Author's Purpose

3. What is this selection mostly about? Main Idea and Details

4. Did you stop to summarize after you read about levers before reading on? How did that help you? Summarize

5. **Look Back and Write** Look back at page 148. How can you use an inclined plane to get a big box onto a truck? Provide evidence to support your answer.

   Key Ideas and Details • Text Evidence

READING STREET ONLINE STORY SORT
www.ReadingStreet.com

Allan Fowler

Allan Fowler has written many science books for beginning readers. He likes to travel and write about different parts of the world.

Mr. Fowler was born in New York, but he lives in Chicago now. He worked in advertising before he became a writer.

Here are other books by Allan Fowler.

Rookie
Read-About Geography
South America
By Allan Fowler

Rookie
Read-About Science
The Top and Bottom of the World
By Allan Fowler

Use the Reading Log in the *Reader's and Writer's Notebook* to record your independent reading.

Common Core State Standards
Writing 1. Write opinion pieces in which they introduce the topic or name the book they are writing about, state an opinion, supply a reason for the opinion, and provide some sense of closure. **Also Language 1.d.**

Persuasive

Let's Write It!

Read Together

Key Features of an Advertisement

- tells what is good about a product or a service
- describes the product or service

READING STREET ONLINE
GRAMMAR JAMMER
www.ReadingStreet.com

Advertisement

An **advertisement,** or ad, tries to get people to use a product or service. The student model on the next page is an example of an advertisement.

Writing Prompt Think about kinds of machines and why people use them. Write an advertisement to get people to use one kind of machine.

Writer's Checklist

Remember, you should . . .

☑ include words to get people to use the machine.

☑ make sure the whole ad is about the machine.

☑ use at least one pronoun.

Look! It Is Cold!

Look at the refrigerators!
They keep food cold and fresh.
A refrigerator is good.
Food will spoil without **it.**

Genre This **advertisement** gives reasons for people to use a refrigerator.

Writing Trait Focus/Ideas All the sentences are about the main idea.

The **pronouns they** and **it** take the place of the words *refrigerators* and *refrigerator.*

Conventions

● **More About Pronouns**

Remember Pronouns take the place of some words in a sentence.

Dad thanks Mom. **He** thanks **her.**

Roy's Wheelchair

by Callen Watkins

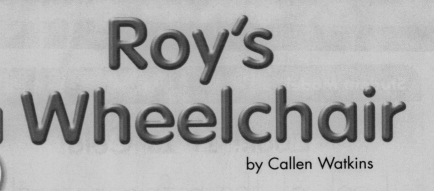

Genre

Literary Nonfiction

- Literary nonfiction tells about real people, animals, places, or events, and often includes photographs.

- Literary nonfiction has a main idea and facts or details that tell more about the main idea.

- Literary nonfiction has some elements of a story, such as characters and setting.

- Read "Roy's Wheelchair." As you read, think about what makes this selection literary nonfiction.

Read Together

Roy uses a wheelchair to get around. He goes all around town with it.

Today Roy is going to the toy store. He uses the ramp to get to the door.

Let's Think About...

How can you tell this selection is literary nonfiction?
Literary Nonfiction

Let's **Think** About...

How does the photograph help explain the words?
Literary Nonfiction

The door is heavy. He pushes against the opener to get in.

Roy uses his wheelchair to go all kinds of places!

Let's **Think** About...

What is the main idea of this selection?
Literary Nonfiction

Let's **Think** About...

Retell the order of events in the text using the words.
Literary Nonfiction

Let's **Think** About...

Reading Across Texts Simple Machines and "Roy's Wheelchair" tell about machines people use. Describe each machine and tell what it does.

Writing Across Texts Write a list of the ways that the machines in Simple Machines and "Roy's Wheelchair" can help people.

Common Core State Standards

Foundational Skills 2.d. Segment spoken single-syllable words into their complete sequence of individual sounds (phonemes).

Phonemic Awareness

Let's Listen for

Sounds

Read Together

- Find the picture of the animal who has drawn a picture. Remove the sound /n/ from the word *drawn*. Say the new word.

- Find five things that are compound words.

- Find something that rhymes with *ball*. Say the sound in the middle of that word. Now say the sound at the end.

**READING STREET ONLINE
SOUND-SPELLING CARDS**
www.ReadingStreet.com

168

Common Core State Standards
Foundational Skills 3. Know and apply grade-level phonics and word analysis skills in decoding words.
Also Foundational Skills 3.g.

Vowel Sound in *ball: aw, au*

Words I Can Blend

s aw

d r aw

f au l t

y aw n e d

h au l

Sentences I Can Read

1. Nicole saw Molly draw with her new marker.

2. It's not my fault that I yawned.

3. Big trucks haul big loads.

170

High-Frequency Words

Words I Can Read

early

learn

science

built

through

Sentences I Can Read

1. We learn to crawl early in life.
2. He saw how our class built this science lab.
3. That fawn jumped through thick brush.

Common Core State Standards
Foundational Skills 3.e. Decode two-syllable words following basic patterns by breaking the words into syllables.
Also Foundational Skills 3., 3.g.

Envision It! | Sounds to Know

oatmeal

digraphs and diphthongs

READING STREET ONLINE
SOUND-SPELLING CARDS
www.ReadingStreet.com

Phonics

Vowel Digraphs and Diphthongs

Words I Can Blend

oa t m ea l

c ow b oy

b oy h oo d

f oo t b a l l

sh ow d ow n

Sentences I Can Read

1. Oatmeal muffins taste good.

2. Tex has liked cowboy boots since his boyhood.

3. This football game is a showdown between those teams.

Science helps us learn safe ways. Early science showed us we can keep raw food safe. Awful things happened when food spoiled. Through science we learn how we can make things.

Sailboats, steamboats, autos, and railroads were built by those who could draw up new plans. Have you seen a countdown for a rocket launch? Pause and thank science for that.

You've learned

- Vowel Sound in *ball: aw, au*
- Syllable Patterns: Vowel Digraphs and Diphthongs

High-Frequency Words

early   learn   science
built   through

Alexander Graham Bell: A Great Inventor

written by Lynne Blanton
illustrated by Guy Francis

Genre

A **biography** is nonfiction text that tells the story of a person's life. Now you will read about Alexander Graham Bell, the man who invented the telephone. What do you want to find out? Set a purpose for reading.

1847
Born in Scotland

1861
Invents wheat "dehusker"

1863
Teaches music at
school for boys

1863
Teaches speech for
deaf children

Alexander Graham Bell was born in Scotland in 1847. His family called him Aleck for short. His mom was deaf. His dad helped deaf boys and girls learn how to speak.

Aleck liked playing music. His mom taught him how to play the piano at an early age. She could not hear, but that did not stop her. She played quite well. Soon Aleck started teaching others how to play.

Aleck's dad helped deaf boys and girls learn to speak well. Aleck liked watching his dad teach. He decided he wanted to teach speech to deaf people too, just like his dad.

As a teen, Aleck liked studying the science of sound. But what he liked best was inventing new things. He daydreamed about things he could make.

Aleck invented a useful tool. It took husks off wheat stalks with a brush. He also built a gadget that made it seem as if his dog could talk!

New Home

1870
Goes to Canada

1871
Goes to Boston

1873
Starts spending more time inventing

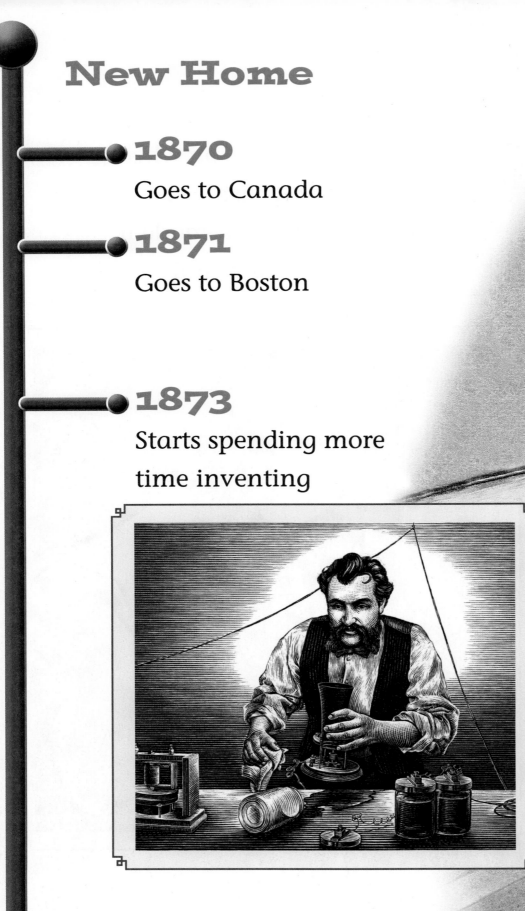

When he was twenty-three, Aleck Bell got awfully sick. He left his boyhood home. He and his family went to Canada. They hoped he would get well in this new place, and he did.

Then Bell went to Boston in the United States. He taught speech for deaf students like his dad did.

Bell liked teaching, but he liked inventing things better. He started spending less time teaching and more time inventing.

Great Idea

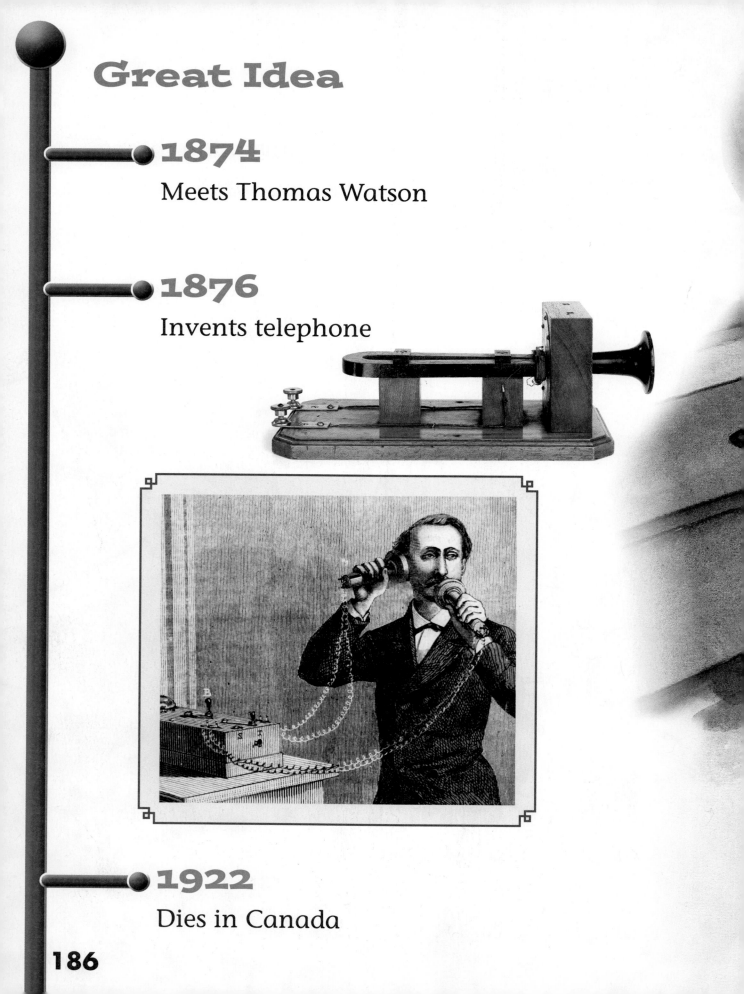

1874
Meets Thomas Watson

1876
Invents telephone

1922
Dies in Canada

One day, while shopping for supplies, Bell met Thomas Watson. Watson, a skillful toolmaker, had helped many inventors before he met Bell. Bell told Watson about his latest plan for a telephone.

Bell and Watson worked long days and nights on Bell's plan. Bell started thinking his plan might succeed. He got a patent for the first telephone. A patent says an inventor owns and can make and sell the thing he or she invents.

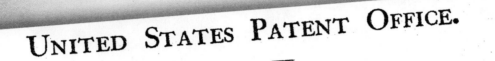

UNITED STATES PATENT OFFICE.

ALEXANDER GRAHAM BELL, OF SALEM, MASSACHUSETTS.

IMPROVEMENT IN TELEGRAPHY.

Specification forming part of Letters Patent No. **174,465**, dated March 7, 1876; application filed February 14, 1876.

To all whom it may concern:
Be it known that I, ALEX BELL, of Salem, Massachuse certain new and useful Imp legraphy, of which the follov tion:
In Letters Patent grante 1875, No. 161,739, I have d of, and apparatus for, tra more telegraphic signals sin a single wire by the emp mitting-instruments, each a succession of electrical in rate from the others; instruments, each tuned t it will be put in vibrati fundamental note by one mitting-instruments; and cuit-breakers operating bratory movement of the ment into a permanent the case may be) of a loc is placed a Morse sounde telegraphic apparatus. described a form of autogr upon the action of the abo ments.
In illustration of my telegraphy I have shown said, as one form of tran an electro-magnet having ture, which is kept in vil of a local battery. This ing makes and breaks t ducing an intermittent c wire. I have found, ho plan the limit to the n can be sent simultaneo wire is very speedily i number of transmitting different rates of vibrati king and breaking

ally breaking the circuit. The current pro- dnced by the latter method I shall term, for

No. 174,465.

A _c_ _d_ _e_ _d_ _c_ _d_
B — — — —
$A+B$ — —— — — —

A — — — —
B — — — — —
$A+B$ — — — — —

A — — — —
B — — — —
$A+B$ — — — —

2 Sheets—Sheet 1.

A. G. BELL.
TELEGRAPHY.

Patented March 7, 1876.

A. G. BELL.
TELEGRAPHY.

No. 174,465.

Fig 6.

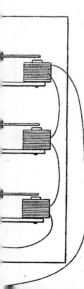

2 Sheets—Sheet 2.

ted March 7, 1876.

The first telephone call took place on March 10, 1876.

That day, Bell dropped a jar by mistake. It spilled and he called for help.

"Mr. Watson, come here. I want you!" he called.

At least, that's how the story goes.

Watson came running. He had heard Bell's voice through the wires! The phone worked!

Bell traveled many places with his telephone. People watched as he showed them how it worked. In a short time, many cities and towns had phones.

Bell kept on inventing things until his death in 1922. He will always keep his place as one of the greatest inventors of all time.

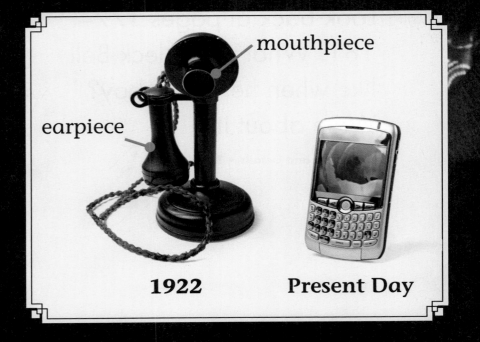

earpiece

mouthpiece

1922   Present Day

Common Core State Standards

Informational Text 1. Ask and answer questions about key details in a text. Also Informational Text 2., 5., Writing 8.

Think Critically

1. Why is Alexander Graham Bell's invention important to people everywhere? Text to World

2. Why do you think the author wanted to tell about Bell and his life? Author's Purpose

3. What happened after Bell and Thomas Watson met? Sequence

4. How do the time lines help you understand Bell's life? Text Structure

5. Look Back and Write Look back at pages 177–181. What was Aleck Bell like when he was a boy? Write about it.

Key Ideas and Details • Text Evidence

Guy Francis

Guy Francis began illustrating at the age of nine when he would draw cartoon characters for his friends. Now he illustrates book covers, children's games, chapter books, and picture books.

Mr. Francis has always liked building, fixing, and creating things. He and his brothers and father even designed and built a cabin on their family ranch.

Mr. Francis loves being an artist and is thrilled to be making a living doing what he loves.

Here are other books illustrated by Guy Francis.

Use the Reading Log in the *Reader's and Writer's Notebook* to record your independent reading.

Let's Write It!

Read Together

Key Features of an Autobiography

- tells about the life of a real person
- the author writes about his or her own life

READING STREET ONLINE
GRAMMAR JAMMER
www.ReadingStreet.com

Narrative

Autobiography

An **autobiography** is a story that an author writes about his or her own life. The student model on the next page is an example of an autobiography.

Writing Prompt Think about some skills that you have. Now write an autobiography that includes these skills.

Writer's Checklist

Remember, you should . . .

☑ write about part of your life, using **I**, **me**, and **my**.

☑ put your sentences in an order that makes sense, from beginning to end.

☑ write and say adverbs to tell how, when, or where.

Baseball and Me

My mom likes baseball. She taught me how to play.

I hit my first ball when I was two. I learned quickly.

Now I am a good player.

I can catch, throw, and bat.

I like baseball too.

Genre
Autobiography
The writer uses the pronouns *I*, *me*, and *my*.

Writing Trait
Sentences
The sentences are all about the writer's idea.

The **adverb** **quickly** tells how the writer learned. **Now** is an adverb of time.

Conventions

- ## Adverbs

Remember An **adverb** can tell how, when, or where an action happens.

I walked **slowly**.   She plays **today**.
He slid **here**.

Common Core State Standards
Informational Text 5. Know and use various text features (e.g., headings, tables of contents, glossaries, electronic menus, icons) to locate key facts or information in a text. **Also Informational Text 6., 7.**

Inventions

21st Century Skills
INTERNET GUY

Read Together

The Internet is full of **Web sites** that are full of information! If you need to write a report or if you want to read more about a topic that interests you, there are many Web sites with the information you need.

- A Web site is a place or an address on the Internet where a World Wide Web document can be found.

- The purpose of a Web site is to find information about a topic. We can check different Web sites.

- Every Web site has text and graphics, but each Web site is organized differently. Take a little time to figure out how.

File   Edit   View   Favorites   Tools   Help

THE HISTORY OF INVENTION

Maude likes science. She wants to learn more about inventions. So she visits an Internet Web site called The History of Invention. Here's what she sees.

Maude clicks on a picture to learn more.

| File | Edit | View | Favorites | Tools | Help |

Cell phone, invented in 1973

Maude reads about early inventions like the telephone and the first airplane ever built. She learns how inventions have changed from the past to the present.

for more practice

Get Online!
www.ReadingStreet.com
Use a Web site to find information about telescopes.

21st Century Skills Online Activity
Log on and follow the step-by-step directions for using a Web site to find more information about the history of telescopes.

Common Core State Standards
Foundational Skills 4.b. Read on-level text orally with accuracy, appropriate rate, and expression on successive readings.
Also Speaking/Listening 4., 5.

Let's **Learn** It!

Read Together

READING STREET ONLINE
VOCABULARY ACTIVITIES
www.ReadingStreet.com

Get Ready For Grade 2

Figure out how techniques in media, such as sound and movement, attract viewers.

Media Literacy

Techniques in Media Television and the Internet are media that have sound and movement. Sound and movement attract the viewer.

Practice It! How would you use sound or movement to attract viewers to a television program or Web site about these topics? Use adverbs as you tell how.

a zoo   **a soccer game**   **the lunchroom**

Vocabulary

A **compound word** is a word made up of two smaller words.

laptop

Laptop is a compound word.

Practice It! Read these words. Write the two words that make up the compound word. Then draw a picture of the compound word.

popcorn   **raindrop**   **crosswalk**

Fluency

Expression and Intonation When you read, try to add emotion to the words. Use your voice to add meaning.

Practice It!

1. Jane mowed the lawn early today.

2. Paul can learn to draw a sailboat.

3. The sauce soaked through the cloth.

Common Core State Standards

Language 6. Use words and phrases acquired through conversations, reading and being read to, and responding to texts, including using frequently occurring conjunctions to signal simple relationships (e.g., *I named my hamster Nibblet because she nibbles too much because she likes that*).

Read Together

Let's Talk About

Ideas That Change Our World

- Recall how we can look at things in a different way.

- Share ideas about what can happen when someone has a new idea.

READING STREET ONLINE
CONCEPT TALK VIDEO
www.ReadingStreet.com

Common Core State Standards
Foundational Skills 2.d. Segment spoken
single-syllable words into their complete
sequence of individual sounds (phonemes).
Also Foundational Skills 2.b.

Phonemic Awareness

Let's Listen for

Read Together

Sounds

● Find the picture of gold
paint. Remove the sound
/g/ from the word *gold*.
Say the new word.

● Find something that
rhymes with *most*.
Say the sound at the
beginning of the word.
Now say the sound in
the middle of the word.

● Find something that
contains the long *i*
sound. Say each sound
in that word.

READING STREET ONLINE
SOUND-SPELLING CARDS
www.ReadingStreet.com

Common Core State Standards
Language 4.b. Use frequently occurring affixes as a clue to the meaning of a word.
Also Foundational Skills 3.c., 3.g.

Envision It! | Sounds to Know

unwrap

prefix un-

replant

prefix re-

READING STREET ONLINE
SOUND-SPELLING CARDS
www.ReadingStreet.com

Phonics

Prefixes *un-, re-*

Words I Can Blend

u n kn ow n

u n m a d e

r e r ea d

u n f e d

r e f i l l

Sentences I Can Read

1. It was unknown whether her bed was left unmade.

2. Reread that note to see if her pet is still unfed.

3. Can you please refill my glass?

Words I Can Read

carry

answered

poor

different

Sentences I Can Read

1. It is unfair that he must carry it by himself.

2. Kim answered that this poor road is uneven.

3. Can you retell three different stories?

I told Mom I must find a way to carry different things. My old backpack can't hold all that I must take.

Mom answered, "Poor child, you can replace books in your pack. Do you unload and refill the pack each day? Are you unable to fit it all? Keep your backpack on your back, but carry most things in your hands."

You've learned

🔄 Prefixes *un-, re-*
🔄 Long *o: o*, Long *i: i*

High-Frequency Words
carry   answered
poor   different

The Stone Garden

written by Chieri Uegaki
illustrated by Miki Sakamoto

 Realistic fiction takes place in a setting that seems real. This story takes place in a yard in a big city.

What can happen when someone has a new idea?

Momoko sat on the steps of her new home. "This yard needs a garden," she told her dog Pochi.

The yard was bordered on all sides with homes like hers. Except for three old tires and a few empty crates, it was as cold and bare as the moon.

The caretaker walked by. "Hello, Momo-girl,"
he said.

"Mr. B., is that your land?"

"That is no man's land," Mr. B. said, "because
no man has the time to do a thing with it."

"May I do something with it?" Momoko asked.

Mr. B. shrugged. "Why not? As long as it does not make more work for me."

The first thing this poor, unwanted yard needed was a cleaning, Momoko decided. So she picked up every bit of litter. She swept and reswept the ground clear.

Then she and Pochi made a game of piling the tires in one corner and taking the crates to another.

Next, she filled her pockets with all
the stones they could carry.

Now she was ready to plant. She used an old spoon her mother gave her to dig a furrow. Into the furrow went the stones, *plop, plop, plop.* She gently covered the stones with earth and watered them with a coffee can. Then she sat down and wished and waited.

By now everyone in the complex was watching her. From behind their curtains, some called her "that silly girl." But they were curious. One by one they came outside.

"I've planted a stone garden," Momoko answered anyone who asked.

"A stone garden! Ha!" said one man. Momoko smiled and kept working. The man returned a while later.

"Here," he said gruffly and handed her a potted yellow pansy.

Momoko thanked him. She replanted the pansy in the ground, and they both stood back to admire it.

Later, a young woman stopped by and asked Momoko what she was doing.

"I've planted a stone garden," she said.

The young woman laughed. But as Momoko continued to weed and water, she too went away and returned with a gift. "They're tulips," she explained, as she offered a bag of bulbs.

Momoko thanked her and planted the bulbs all over the yard.

One morning, Momoko found that someone had buried the three unused tires along one side of the yard. Inside each tire was a tiny rosebush.

The next day, she found two empty crates refilled with dirt. One crate held several young tomato plants. The other had two markers in it. One said "carrots." The other said "peas."

And so it went. Every day something was different. Mr. B. lent Momoko a hose. A pair of little apple trees appeared. One day a neighbor left a butterfly bush with red blossoms. A basket of herbs showed up beside the vegetable crates with a small stone lion to protect it.

As the stone garden grew, Momoko met more and more of her neighbors. Chairs popped up like mushrooms outside people's front doors. In the evenings, people would sit and visit. Some would help Momoko take care of the garden.

Momoko loved the trees and shrubs and flowers. But she was most excited about the vegetables. She almost burst with happiness when one mild morning, it happened. A tender sprout unwound itself and poked its head out of the soft dirt.

"Oh," Momoko cried. She ran to share
the news.

Everyone came out to see this small miracle.

"Who would have believed it?" said Mr. B. "Who would have believed you could grow such a garden here?"

Momoko knelt down to gaze at all the living green things. Who would have believed what you could grow from a pocketful of stones?

Common Core State Standards
Literature 1. Ask and answer questions
about key details in a text.
Also Literature 2., Writing 5.

Envision It! | Retell

Think Critically

Read Together

1. Pretend you have a garden. What would you plant in it? Why? Text to Self

2. How does the author show how Momoko's neighborhood has changed? Think Like an Author

3. What does this story teach you about communities? Theme

4. Why did everyone first laugh at Momoko's garden? Inferring

5. Look Back and Write Look back at pages 224–226. What grew in Momoko's stone garden? Write about it. Use evidence from the story to support your answer.

Key Ideas and Details • Text Evidence

Meet the Author

Chieri Uegaki

Chieri Uegaki began writing stories when she was seven years old. Her father had a copy machine at home, so Ms. Uegaki was able to print her own family newspaper. She remembers writing one story for the paper about a grape named Gary and how he became a raisin.

Here is another book by Chieri Uegaki.

Use the Reading Log in the *Reader's and Writer's Notebook* to record your independent reading.

233

Common Core State Standards

Writing 1. Write opinion pieces in which they introduce the topic or name the book they are writing about, state an opinion, supply a reason for the opinion, and provide some sense of closure. **Also Language 1., 1.i., 2.b.**

Let's Write It!

Read Together

Key Features of a Poem

- many are shorter than a story
- often the lines end with rhyming words

**READING STREET ONLINE
GRAMMAR JAMMER
www.ReadingStreet.com**

Descriptive

Poem

A **poem** can describe things or express your imagination. The student model on the next page is an example of a poem.

Writing Prompt Think about something old that you could make into something new. Now write a poem about how to make it new.

Writer's Checklist

Remember, you should . . .

- ☑ tell how to make an old thing new.
- ☑ write a poem and use end punctuation for sentences.
- ☑ use one or more prepositional phrases.

Sock Puppets

Put an old sock on your hand.

Make it a singer in a puppet band!

Add buttons for eyes and yarn for hair.

Aren't you glad socks come in a pair?

Genre
This **poem** has rhyming words: **hand, band** and **hair, pair.**

A **preposition, on,** starts the **prepositional phrase on your hand.** Say the whole phrase.

Writing Trait Conventions
The complete sentences end with correct punctuation.

Conventions

- ## Prepositions

  Remember In, on, at, with, to, and **for** are **prepositions**. A preposition starts a **prepositional phrase,** such as **in a cup**.

Common Core State Standards
Literature 10. With prompting and support, read prose and poetry of appropriate complexity for grade 1. **Also Literature 4.**

Genre
Poetry

Read Together

- A poem may tell a story, or it may express the poet's feelings about something.

- Poems are written in lines and stanzas. Poems usually have rhyme and rhythm.

- Some poems have alliteration, or words with the same beginning sound.

- Read the poems. As you read, listen for rhyme, rhythm, and alliteration.

Common Language

My new friend spoke to
   me in French,
And I couldn't tell what she said.
When I tried to answer her,
She only shook her head.
Suddenly both of us laughed,
And it was then we found
The wonderful language
   of laughter
Is known the wide world round!

by Helen Pettigrew
illustrated by Tuesday Mourning

236

Skyscraper

by Dennis Lee
illustrated by Dan Santat

Skyscraper, skyscraper,
Scrape me some sky:
Tickle the sun
While the stars go by.

Tickle the stars
While the sun's climbing high,
Then skyscraper, skyscraper,
Scrape me some sky.

Let's Think About...

What is the **alliteration** in the last two lines of "Common Language"?

Let's Think About...

Clap the **rhythm** in "Skyscraper."

237

A Map and a Dream

by Karen O'Donnell Taylor
illustrated by Judy Stead

Let's **Think** About...

What are the **rhyming** words in this poem?

Maps are more
than tiny lines
intersecting
lace designs . . .
More than names
and colored dots,
rivers, mountains,
tourist spots.
Maps are keys
to secret places
vast new worlds
and unknown faces.
I can trace each
graceful line . . .

Orange Groves

BIG SHOE

MOTEL

Painted Desert

"Bennie"

Close my eyes
and in my mind
I can travel
anywhere . . .
A map, a dream
can take me there!

Old Faithful

Big Blue Lake

Tumbleweeds

Let's Think About...

Is the poet telling a story or expressing her feelings about something? How do you know?

Let's Think About...

Reading Across Texts What is Momoko's idea in *The Stone Garden*? What ideas do the poets write about in the three poems? How do all of these ideas change things?

Writing Across Texts Write a poem about Momoko's garden. You might describe how it is created, what it looks like at the end, or how Momoko feels about it. Use rhyme, rhythm, and alliteration.

239

Common Core State Standards
Speaking/Listening 5. Add drawings or other visual displays to descriptions when appropriate to clarify ideas, thoughts, and feelings. **Also Foundational Skills 4.b., Language 1.i.**

Let's **Learn** It!

Read Together

READING STREET ONLINE
VOCABULARY ACTIVITIES
www.ReadingStreet.com

Get Ready For Grade 2

Think about ways in which you can respond to media.

Media Literacy

Respond to Media One way to respond to media is to draw a picture or write about what we see, hear, or read. We can respond in a way that shows how we feel, what we learned, or what we liked.

Practice It! Look at a school lunch menu. Draw pictures for two items. Say and write sentences for each picture. Include prepositional phrases.

240

Vocabulary

Time and order words tell when things happen.

today   **tomorrow**

Today and *tomorrow* are time and order words.

Practice It! Read these words. Use them to tell a story.

first   **next**   **then**   **later**

Fluency

Appropriate Phrasing When you read, punctuation marks tell you when to pause, show excitement, raise your voice, or stop.

Practice It!

1. I answered the most questions!

2. Will you redo it in a different way?

3. We will carry the poor dog home.

axles • buried

Aa

axles **Axles** are bars on which wheels turn.

Bb

borrowed If you **borrowed** something, you got it from a person or a place just for a while. I **borrowed** books from the library.

breath **Breath** is air taken into and sent out of the lungs. Take a deep **breath.**

buried When something is **buried,** it is covered up with dirt. The dog dug up the bone that it had **buried** last week.

buried

bush A **bush** is a woody plant that is smaller than a tree.

Cc

curious When a person is **curious,** that person wants to find out about something. Simon was **curious** about the new books in the library.

Dd

dehusker A **dehusker** is a machine that removes the dry outer covering, or husk, from a grain.

detectives **Detectives** are police officers or other people who work at solving mysteries.

disagreed If you and a friend **disagreed,** that means both had different ideas.

disagreed

favorite • hey

Ff

favorite Your **favorite** thing is the one you like better than all the others. What is your **favorite** flower?

Hh

heard When you have **heard** something, you have taken in sounds through your ears. He **heard** the noise.

heard

hey **Hey** is a word you use to get someone's attention.

hurray **Hurray** is what you shout when you are very happy. Give a **hurray** for our team!

hurray

Ii

inclined plane An **inclined plane** is a plank or other flat surface placed at an angle and used to move heavy things to a higher place. It is a simple machine.

Ll

lawn mower A **lawn mower** is a machine people use to cut grass.

machines • million

Mm

machines **Machines** are things with moving parts that do work for you. Cars, washers, and computers are **machines**.

meadow A **meadow** is a piece of land where grass grows. There are sheep in the **meadow.**

meadow

million A **million** is a very large number. It is also written as 1,000,000.

miracle A **miracle** is something marvelous or almost unbelievable that happens. It was a **miracle** that the boat didn't sink.

mystery A **mystery** is something that is hard to understand. It was a **mystery** why the radio started playing in the middle of the night.

Nn

neighbors **Neighbors** are people who live next door to or near you. Marcus likes to visit with his **neighbors.**

neighbors

piano • presently

Pp

piano A **piano** is a large musical instrument that you sit at and play with your fingers.

potato bugs **Potato bugs** are beetles that eat the leaves of the potato plant.

potato bug

presently **Presently** means at the present time, or now. She is **presently** in first grade.

pulley A **pulley** is a wheel with ropes that helps lift things.

pulley

Ss

Scotland **Scotland** is a country north of England.

solve When you **solve** something, you find the answer to it. The detective will **solve** the mystery by using the clues.

solved • telephone

solved **Solved** is the past tense of *solve*.

surface A **surface** is the top part or outside of something. The **surface** of the road was very wet after the rain.

surface

Tt

telephone

telephone A **telephone** is something you use to talk to people far away. Please answer the **telephone** if it rings.

tippy-toe **Tippy-toe** means on the tips of your toes. The girl walked **tippy-toe** so that she would not wake her baby brother.

tippy-toe

Uu

usually If something **usually** happens, it happens very often or almost all the time. We **usually** eat dinner at six o'clock.

vacuum • vegetables

Vv

vacuum A **vacuum** cleaner is a machine you can use to clean rugs, curtains, and floors.

vacuum

vegetables **Vegetables** are plants that have parts that we use for food. Peas, corn, beets, and green beans are all **vegetables.**

vegetables

Yy

young People are **young** before they are grown up.

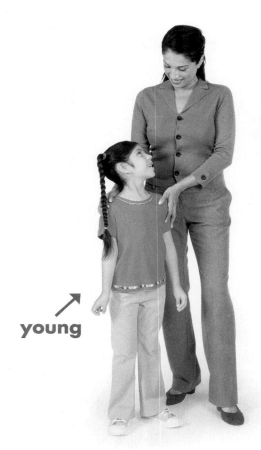

young

Tippy-Toe Chick, GO!

along
behind
eyes
never
pulling
toward

Dot & Jabber and the Great Acorn Mystery

among
another
instead
none

Mole and the Baby Bird

door
loved
should
wood

Simple Machines

against
goes
heavy
kinds
today

The Stone Garden

answered
carry
different
poor

Alexander Graham Bell: A Great Inventor

built
early
learn
science
through

Aa Bb Cc

Dd Ee Ff

Gg Hh Ii

Jj Kk Ll

Mm Nn Oo

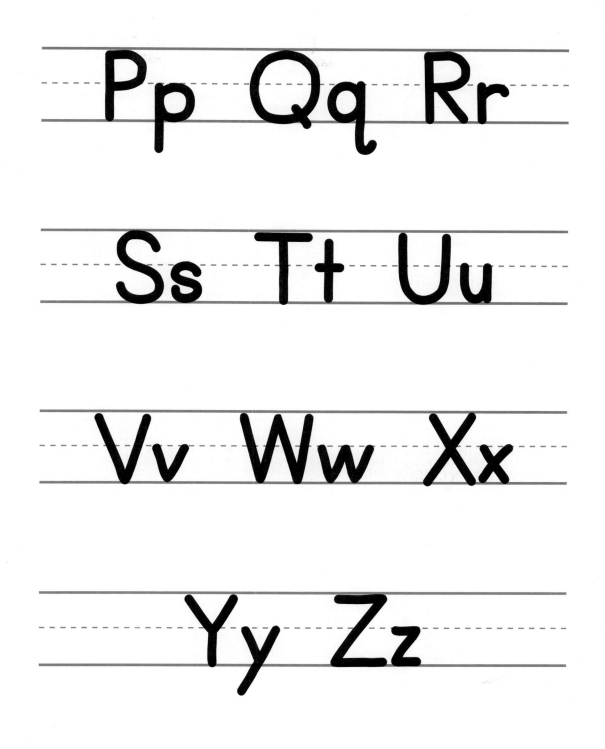

Pp Qq Rr

Ss Tt Uu

Vv Ww Xx

Yy Zz

Acknowledgments

Text

Grateful acknowledgment is made to the following for copyrighted material:

HarperCollins Publishers

"Tippy-Toe-Chick, Go!" By George W.B. Shannon. Text copyright © 2003 George W. B. Shannon. Illustrations by Laura Dronzek. Illustrations copyright © 2003, Laura Dronzek. Used by permission of HarperCollins Publishers, Inc.

Bloomsbury USA

"Mole and the Baby Bird" by Marjorie Newman copyright © 2002. Illustrations copyright © 2002 by Patrick Benson. Used by permission of Bloomsbury USA. All rights reserved.

Houghton Mifflin Harcourt Publishing Company

Dot & Jabber And The Great Acorn Mystery by Ellen Stoll Walsh. Copyright © 2001 by Ellen Stoll Walsh. Reproduced by permission of Houghton Mifflin Harcourt Publishing Company. All rights reserved.

Highlights for Children

"Common Language" by Helen Pettigrew from *A School Year Of Poems,* selected by Walter B. Barbe, Ph.D. Copyright © 2005 by Highlights for Children, Inc., Columbus, Ohio. Used by permission of Highlights for Children.

Westwood Creative Artists Ltd.

"Skyscraper" from *Alligator Pie* by Dennis Lee (Macmillan of Canada, 1974; Key Porter Books, 2001). Copyright © 1974 Dennis Lee. With permission of the author.

Karen O'Donnell Taylor

"A Map and a Dream" by Karen O'Donnell Taylor from *Got Geography!* Used by permission.

Note: Every effort has been made to locate the copyright owner of material reproduced on this component. Omissions brought to our attention will be corrected in subsequent editions.

Cover: (B) ©Theo Allots/Getty Images, (T) Getty Images

Illustrations

EI2-EI9 Mary Anne Lloyd; **EI12-EI21** Chris Lensch; **14-15** Robbie Short; **44-49** Constanza Basaluzzo; **54-55, 174-192** Guy Francis; **82-87** Ken Gamage; **92-93** Liisa Guida; **132-133** O'Kif; **168-169** Jennifer Zivoin; **204-205** Stephen Gilpin; **210-231** Miki Sakamoto; **236** Tuesday Mourning; **237** Dan Santat; **238-239** Judy Stead

Photographs

Every effort has been made to secure permission and provide appropriate credit for photographic material. The publisher deeply regrets any omission and pledges to correct errors called to its attention in subsequent editions.

Unless otherwise acknowledged, all photographs are the property of Pearson Education, Inc.

Photo locators denoted as follows: Top (T), Center (C), Bottom (B), Left (L), Right (R), Background (Bkgd)

4, 10 (Bkgd) ©Adam Jones/Getty Images, (L) ©Xavier Bonghi/Getty Images; **12** (Bkgd) Ghislain & Marie David de Lossy/Image Bank/Getty Images; **13** (BR) Andy Roberts/Stone/Getty Images, (C) Getty Images; **16** (B) ©Arco Images GmbH/Alamy Images, (T) ©Tim Davis/Corbis; **50** (BL) ©DK Images; **53** (B) AP/Wide World Photos; **56** (BC) ©Arco Images GmbH/Alamy Images, (B) ©Big Cheese Photo LLC/Alamy, (C) ©Ron Chapple Stock/Alamy, (T) ©Terrance Klassen/Alamy, (TC) ©Tim Davis/Corbis; **58** (T) ©Gary Vestal/Getty Images, (C) Getty Images; **90** (T) ©John Cancalosi/Nature Picture Library, (Bkgd) Image Source/Getty Images, (B) Purestock/Jupiter Images; **96** (T) ©Julia Fishkin/The Image Bank/Getty Images, (B) ©Tim Pannell/Jupiter Images; **129** BananaStock/Jupiter Images; **131** (TL) ©Tom Stewart/Corbis; **134** (B) ©Photo Network/Alamy Images; **136** (T) ©Bill Losh/Getty Images, (B) ©Fred Kris/Alamy Images; **138** (B) Corbis; **139** ©Ross Whitaker/Getty Images; **140** (T) Corbis, (B) Jupiter Images; **143** ©Tony Freeman/PhotoEdit; **144** ©Michelle D. Bridwell/PhotoEdit; **146** (B) ©Dennis MacDonald/PhotoEdit, (TL) ©Kayte M. Deioma/PhotoEdit, (TR) ©Royalty-Free/Corbis; **147** Stock Boston; **148** (B) ©Bonnie Kamin/PhotoEdit, (T) ©David Young-Wolff/PhotoEdit; **149** ©David Forbert/SuperStock; **150** Stephen Gibson/Shutterstock; **151** (T) ©Francis & Donna Caldwell/Affordable Photo Stock, (B) ©Royalty-Free/Corbis; **152** Stock Boston; **153** (BR) ©Laurence Monneret/Getty Images, (TL) ©Mary Kate Denny/PhotoEdit; **154** Stock Boston; **155** (TL) ©Tom Stewart/Corbis, (BL) ©George Shelley/Corbis, (BR) ©Tom Stewart/Corbis, (TR) ©Jennie Woodcock/Reflections Photolibrary/Corbis; **158** (BL) Stock Boston; **166** (B) ©Owen Edelsten/Masterfile Corporation; **167** (BR) ©Bettmann/Corbis, (T) ©Science Source/Photo Researchers, Inc.; **170** (B) ©John Garrett/Getty Images, (T) ©Mira/Alamy Images; **182** ©Antar Dayal/Illustration Works/Corbis; **186** (TC) Clive Streeter/Courtesy of The Science Museum, London/©DK Images; **188** (T, C, B) U.S. Patent and Trademark Office; **193** (Bkgd) ©Randy Faris/Corbis, (BR) Corbis, (BR) Mark Hamilton/©DK Images; **200** Getty Images; **201** Jeffrey Coolidge/Getty Images; **202** (Bkgrd) ©Anna Peisl/zefa/Corbis, (T) ©Jennie Woodcock/Reflections Photolibrary/Corbis, (BL) ©Jose Luis Pelaez, Inc./Corbis; **206** (T) ©Michael Heinsen/Getty Images, (B) Alamy; **208** (B) ©LWA-Sharie Kennedy/Corbis, (T) ©Stockxpert; **242** ©Margo Harrison/Shutterstock; **243** ©Ariel Skelley/Corbis; **244** ©Ianni Dimitrov/Alamy Images; **246** Getty Images; **247** ©Ed Bock/Corbis; **248** ©Royalty-Free/Corbis; **249** Stock Boston; **250** (C) ©Royalty-Free/Corbis; **251** Getty Images; **252** Corbis; **255** Stock Boston

Identify and read the high-frequency words that you have learned this year. Look how many words you can read!

Unit R.1
a
green
I
see

Unit R.2
like
one
the
we

Unit R.3
do
look
was
yellow
you

Unit R.4
are
have
that
they
two

Unit R.5
he
is
three
to
with

Unit R.6
for
go
here
me
where

Unit 1.1
come
in
my
on
way

Unit 1.2
she
take
up
what

Unit 1.3
blue
from
get
help
little
use

Unit 1.4
eat
five
four

her
this
too

Unit 1.5
saw
small
tree
your

Unit 1.6
home
into
many
them

Unit 2.1
catch
good
no
put
said
want

Unit 2.2
be
could
horse
of
old
paper

Unit 2.3
live
out
people
who
work

Unit 2.4
down
inside
now
there
together

Unit 2.5
around
find
food
grow
under
water

Unit 2.6
also
family
new
other
some
their

High-Frequency Words

Unit 3.1
always
become
day
everything
nothing
stays
things

Unit 3.2
any
enough
ever
every
own
sure
were

Unit 3.3
away
car
friends
house
our
school
very

Unit 3.4
afraid
again
few
how
read
soon

Unit 3.5
done
know
push
visit
wait

Unit 3.6
before
does
good-bye
oh
right
won't

Unit 4.1
about
enjoy
give
surprise
worry
would

Unit 4.2
colors
draw
drew
great
over
show
sign

Unit 4.3
found
mouth

once
took
wild

Unit 4.4
above
eight
laugh
moon
touch

Unit 4.5
picture
remember
room
stood
thought

Unit 4.6
across
because
dance
only
opened
shoes
told

Unit 5.1
along
behind
eyes
never
pulling
toward

Unit 5.2
door
loved
should
wood

Unit 5.3
among
another
instead
none

Unit 5.4
against
goes
heavy
kinds
today

Unit 5.5
built
early
learn
science
through

Unit 5.6
answered
carry
different
poor